The Ultimate Self-Teaching Method! Level One

Play Banjo Today!

A Complete Guide to the Basics

T0084234

To access audio visit:
www.halleonard.com/mylibrary

Enter Code
7767-7235-8108-1518

by Colin O'Brien

Recording Credits:
Colin O'Brien, Banjo, Guitar & Narration
Recorded at Buckaroo Studios,
Milwaukee, WI

ISBN 978-1-4234-1993-8

HAL•LEONARD®

Visit Hal Leonard Online at
www.halleonard.com

Contact us:
Hal Leonard
7777 West Bluemound Road
Milwaukee, WI 53213
Email: info@halleonard.com

In Europe, contact:
Hal Leonard Europe Limited
42 Wigmore Street
Marylebone, London, W1U 2RN
Email: info@halleonardeurope.com

In Australia, contact:
Hal Leonard Australia Pty. Ltd.
4 Lentara Court
Cheltenham, Victoria, 3192 Australia
Email: info@halleonard.com.au

Introduction

Track 1

Welcome to *Play Banjo Today!* This beginner's book will guide you step by step to playing songs on your banjo in the popular and exciting bluegrass style.

About the Audio

All the music written in this book is also on the Audio. Each audio example has a track number that appears in the book next to the written music. Check out bonus Tracks 96 and 97 to hear a full performance of the banjo classic "Cripple Creek." Listening to the songs is so important that it actually counts as practice! When you can hear the song in your mind's ear, it will make learning it from the written music easier, faster, and more enjoyable.

About the Author

Author Colin O'Brien travels throughout the U.S.A. performing concerts and presenting banjo workshops. He has won several awards for his solo concerts and recordings which feature his banjo, fiddle, guitar, and his amazing foot percussion. He'd love to hear from you! *www.colingobrien.com*

Contents

Meet the Banjo

Track 2

The first banjos in America were brought from Africa in the late 1600s. They were made from gourds and animal hides. These banjos could be considered the great-grandfathers of the banjo you have. Though the African banjos were very different from the one you're learning to play, you'll still see some similarities: the round body covered with a skin, and the neck and strings attached at the back of the body.

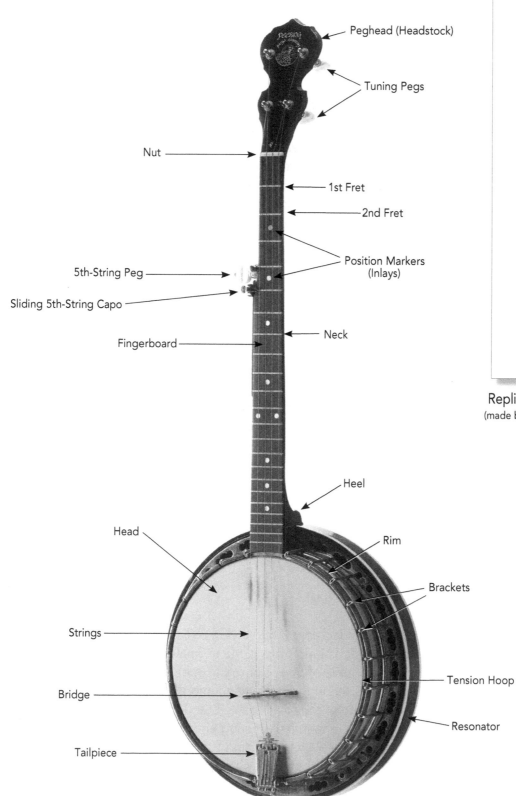

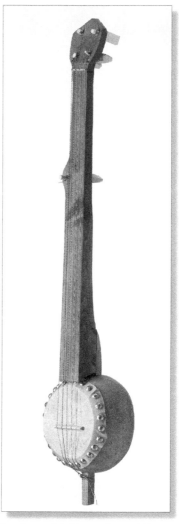

Replica of African Gourd Banjo
(made by Mike Gregory, www.littlebanjos.lunare.net)

Peghead (Headstock)

Tuning Pegs

Nut

1st Fret

2nd Fret

Position Markers (Inlays)

5th-String Peg

Sliding 5th-String Capo

Fingerboard

Neck

Heel

Head

Rim

Brackets

Strings

Tension Hoop

Bridge

Resonator

Tailpiece

How to Hold Your Banjo

The Strap

Even if you're sitting, it's very important to have a strap! There are straps made for banjos, but in most cases a guitar strap will work just fine. If you are using a guitar strap, you'll need to tie it onto the bracket hooks at the location shown.

Sitting

Sitting is the most comfortable position when first learning to play. Most of the weight of the banjo can rest in your lap. The strap should be pulled tight over your left shoulder (if you're playing right-handed) so there's no slack in the strap between where it leaves your shoulder and the banjo. This will prevent the neck from sliding down from its own weight. You should be able to sit with no hands on your banjo with the strap keeping the peghead about shoulder height.

Standing

Most players adjust their straps so that the bridge of the banjo is about belly-button height.

Puttin' on the Picks

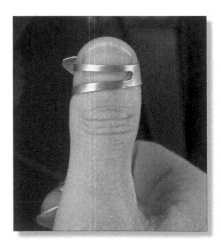

To play banjo in the three-finger bluegrass picking style you'll need two *finger picks* and a *thumb pick*. Thumb picks come in small, medium, and large sizes and are made of plastic or metal (metal pick shown). You'll find that if you try on three plastic thumb picks labeled the same size at a music store, they'll all feel a little different. Try a bunch on until you find one that fits just snug enough to not slip around your thumb when you push on the tip of the pick, which is the part that will be contacting the string when you play. Metal thumb picks can be bent to fit.

Metal finger picks come in one size and need to be bent to fit comfortably around your index and middle fingers. Many players bend the tips back too, so they curve around the tip of the finger. On the finger picks you'll see a number that tells you the *thickness* of the metal. Start with a .15 or .18-size finger pick.

It will take some time for you to get used to the feeling of having picks on. Make sure they are *comfortable*. Everyone's fingers are different, so bend those finger picks around until you find the right shape for your fingers.

Right- and Left-Hand Position

We'll use the terms "pick hand" and "fret hand" throughout this book to accommodate right- and left-handed-players. Left-handed players will need to think of the pictures as if they were looking in a mirror instead of at another player.

Pick Hand

Pick-hand fingers are identified as follows:

> T = Thumb
> I = Index
> M = Middle

The ring finger or pinky (or both) should always lightly rest on the banjo head. This will help stabilize the pick hand when it is picking the strings. Remember to keep both hands relaxed. When playing, both hands are curved as they would be when holding an orange.

Picking closer to the bridge gives you a crisper sound, and picking toward where the neck meets the body gives you a mellower sound.

Fretting Hand

Fret-hand fingers are usually identified by the numbers 1 through 4.

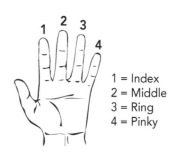

1 = Index
2 = Middle
3 = Ring
4 = Pinky

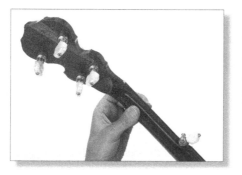

The fret-hand thumb should rest on the center of the back of the neck, as if you're giving a thumb-print.

Your fret-hand fingertips are what touch the strings.

This is a picture of what not to do: don't wrap your hand around the neck like it's a baseball bat. Make sure not to mash your palm against the bottom of the neck.

Make sure there's always room for a pencil to fit between the neck and your palm.

Tuning

Track 3

Tuning to the Audio

Tuning to the notes on the audio is a great way to teach your ears to find the right notes. When you can tell the string you're tuning on your banjo sounds different in pitch from the string played on the audio, your ears are doing their job. The next step is to ask; does your note sound higher or lower than the note on the audio? If you can't tell, tune the string lower until you're certain it's too low, and then tune it higher until it sounds like the note on the audio. This is tuning "up to" the note. After all, we tend to say "let's tune up!" and not "let's tune down." Strings tuned up to the correct pitch will stay in tune longer than if you were to tune down to the pitch.

G Tuning

The G tuning is the most common tuning used for three-finger picking. Strings are tuned to the pitches G–D–G–B–D, and are numbered 5–4–3–2–1.

String 1 is closest to the floor. Strings should be tuned from the lowest in pitch to the highest, meaning you'll start with string 4. On the audio at 1:40, you'll hear the strings played in this order:

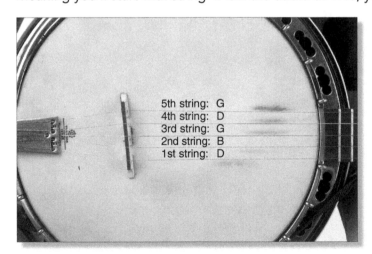

5th string: G
4th string: D
3rd string: G
2nd string: B
1st string: D

- Fourth string, D. This is the thickest string.

- Third string, G.

- Second string, B.

- First string, D. This one is closest to the floor.

- Fifth string, G. This is the short string.

Tuning to a Piano

You can also tune your banjo using a piano. This is similar to tuning to the audio. If your piano has foot pedals, find the pedal that makes the piano notes continue ringing after you strike them; this way you can tune the banjo to the ringing piano note. Like tuning to the audio, this is tuning *by ear*.

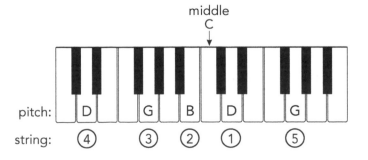

middle C

pitch: D G B D G

string: ④ ③ ② ① ⑤

Using an Electronic Tuner

Electronic tuners are available at most music stores. Using a tuner lets you see when you're in tune. Get one to use as your number 2 tuning tool. What's your number 1 tuning tool? Your ears! If you try tuning to a piano or the audio and simply can't get it to sound right, *then* use your tuner, and it will show you whether a string is flat (too low) or sharp (too high). Listen while using it and learn from what it tells you!

Relative Tuning

If you're stuck on a desert island with nothing but an out-of-tune banjo, you can still tune it! Here's how:

1. Tune the 4th string (the low D, the thickest string) to a piano, pitch pipe, electronic tuner, or the audio. If none of these are available, approximate D as best you can.

2. Press the 4th string at the 5th fret. This is G. Tune the open 3rd string to this pitch.

3. Press the 3rd string at the 4th fret. This is B. Tune the open 2nd string to this pitch.

4. Press the 2nd string at the 3rd fret. This is D. Tune the open first string to this pitch.

5. Press the 1st string down at the 5th fret. This is G. Tune the open 5th string (short string) to this pitch.

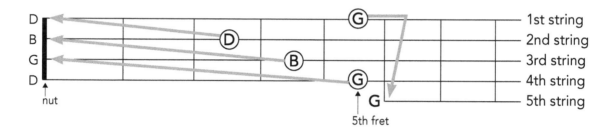

Tuning Tips

- Always play the string just before turning its tuning peg. This way you'll be able to hear the change in pitch as you're turning the peg.

- Be sure to turn the peg slowly so you can concentrate on the changes in pitch.

- Always tune *up to pitch* from below. If it is too high, first tune down past the target pitch.

- Whatever method you use to tune, it's important to listen. With experience, your ears will become your most reliable tuners. They're very portable, and hard to forget!

How to Read Tablature

Track 4

The five lines you see here are called **tab staff lines**. Each represents one of your banjo strings. The line on the bottom is the short G string. The next line up is the D string, the thickest string on the banjo. The middle line is the second G string. The next is the B string, and finally, the top line is the second D string, which is the string closest to the floor.

Below you'll see some numbers on the staff lines. They tell you which fret and which string to press down with your fretting hand. Occasionally throughout this book you'll also see numbers above the staff lines, as shown in the examples below. These numbers tell you which *fret-hand* finger to use to play that note.

Here you put your index finger on the first fret of the B string.

► Notice in all of the pictures that the fingers play just behind the fret, though we use the word "on." This is the area where you'll get the best tone with the smallest effort. This is where you should always play!

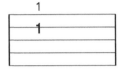

Here you put your third finger on the second fret of the D string.

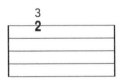

This note is on the thick D string. The second finger goes on the second fret.

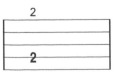

Rhythm

Rhythm tells you two things about notes: when to play them, and how long they last.

Quarter Notes

The staff below is divided into three **measures**. In this book, each measure contains four **beats**. In each measure below there are four **quarter notes**, indicated by a vertical **stem**. Each quarter note lasts for one beat. Just like there are four quarters to a dollar, four quarter notes can fit into a measure. Play the notes below (all are on the middle G string) with your pick-hand thumb, indicated here and throughout the book by a "T" below the note. Your thumb picks in a downward motion. Keep your pinky and ring fingers touching the head as you pick to help you get even rhythm and tone.

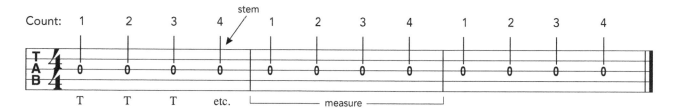

Track 5

> ▶ Playing with a smooth, even rhythm is very important!

Eighth Notes

The most common note value in banjo music is the **eighth note**, designated by the **beams** connecting the stems into groups of four notes. Eight eighth notes fit into each measure. Below are three measures filled with eighth notes. Play these notes on the G string with your pick-hand thumb and count "1 and 2 and 3 and 4 and" as you play.

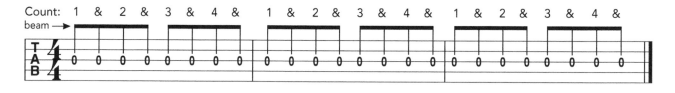

Track 6

Whole Notes

You will occasionally see **whole notes**, usually at the end of a piece. In rhythmic tablature, we write whole notes with just one fret number in the measure. Like their name implies, they take up a whole measure. Count "one, two, three, four" aloud, plucking the string on beat one and letting it ring for the full four beats.

Track 7

Reading Exercises

The exercises below are played with the thumb (T), index finger (I), and middle finger (M).

This first short exercise is to be played with the thumb. The count written above the staff will help you keep an even rhythm. Count aloud as you play.

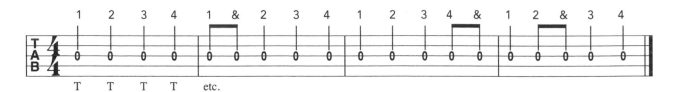

Track 8

Now it's time to get the pick-hand fingers in on the act. The fingers pick in an upward motion. 90% of the fingers' motion happens from the middle knuckle of the finger. Be sure to keep your pinky or ring finger resting on the banjo head.

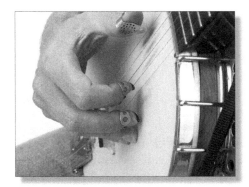

Picking the B String: Setup

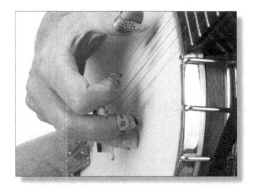

Picking the B String: Follow Through

Play the following notes with your index finger. Keep the hand nice and steady.

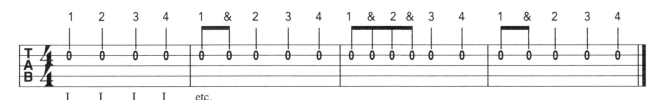

Track 9

This one on the high D string is to be played with the middle finger.

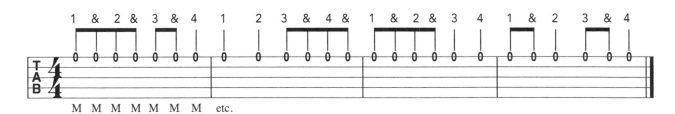

Track 10

Here's one using all of the picking fingers.

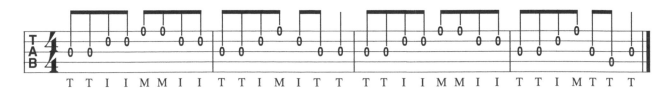

Track 11

Pinching & Chord Basics

A *pinch* involves picking two or three notes at the same time. Be careful not to pull the pinky and/or ring finger away from the banjo head when executing a pinch. Listen to the audio to hear the simultaneous notes.

Thumbin' the Gs

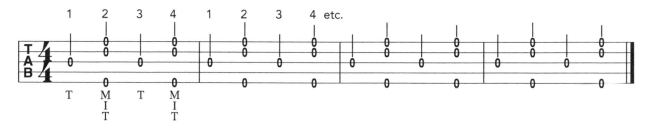

This is the same thing, but now the thumb plays the low D string.

Thumbin' the Low D

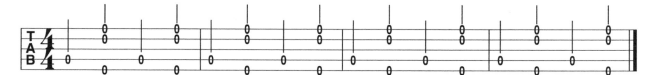

Now the thumb alternates between the G and D strings—hence the title.

Switch Hittin' (Alternating Thumb)

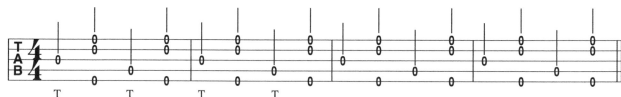

Here's one leading with the index finger. Notice the pinches now only have two notes in them, not three.

Index in the Lead

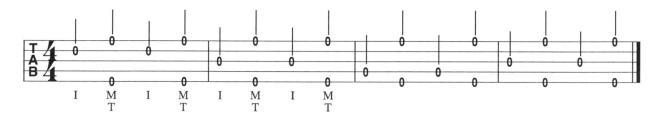

Open-Position Chords

With just three chords, G, C, and D7, you can play many songs on the banjo. The banjo is already tuned to a G chord, so you don't even need your fretting hand for that one! Here are the G, C, and D7 chords in what's called **open position**, the lowest possible position for these chords, which includes at least one open string. The fret-hand fingers are shown beneath the **chord frame**, a type of diagram used for stringed instruments. The thick line across the top represents the nut of the banjo. The chords are also shown in tablature form. When playing the G chord, the fretting hand is like a baseball player waiting for the pitch. It's ready to play with the fingers always curved toward the strings. Strum the chords with the thumb. The thumb brushes toward the floor. Don't strum the short G string on the D7 chord.

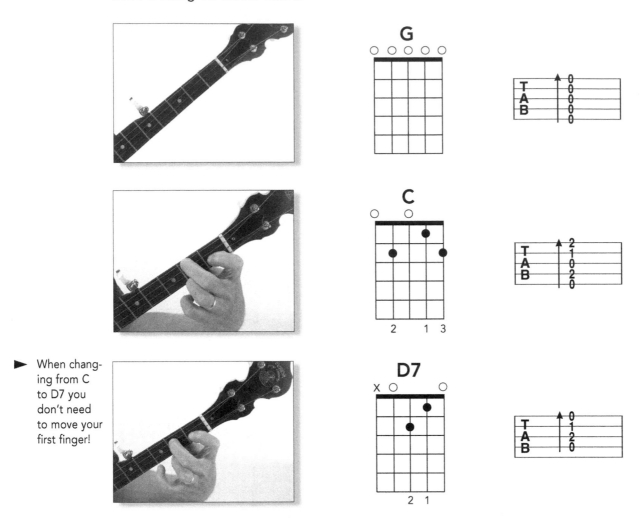

► When changing from C to D7 you don't need to move your first finger!

Now it's time to play some tunes! Here are a few using the pinch you learned.

Notice the direction in the first measure to play the pinch with the thumb, index, and middle finger. The same fingering applies for all the pinches. The last measure of the tune contains **half notes**. Each one of these notes lasts for two beats; the first note is played on beat 1, and the pinch after it is played on beat 3 of the last measure. Count "one, two" for the first half note and "three, four" for the second stack of three.

Hello Banjo

Track 18

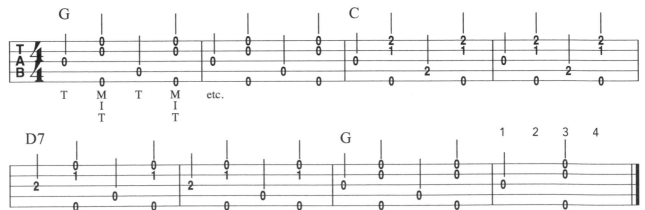

Track 19

Playing Melodies

The *melody* is what you sing or whistle walking down the street, and it's also what you want to hear when playing the banjo. In the next song, the words are under the melody notes.

Goodnight Ladies

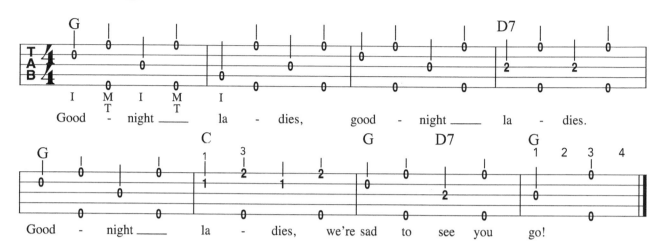

Fingering Tip

When you see a chord symbol such as C or D7, hold the full chord down with the fret hand, even if some of those notes are not supposed to be plucked.

In this tune, you play on the 3rd fret for the first time. The numbers above the staff indicate fret-hand fingering: 1 for index, 2 for middle, 3 for ring finger, and 4 for pinky.

Track 20

Frère Jacques (Are You Sleeping?)

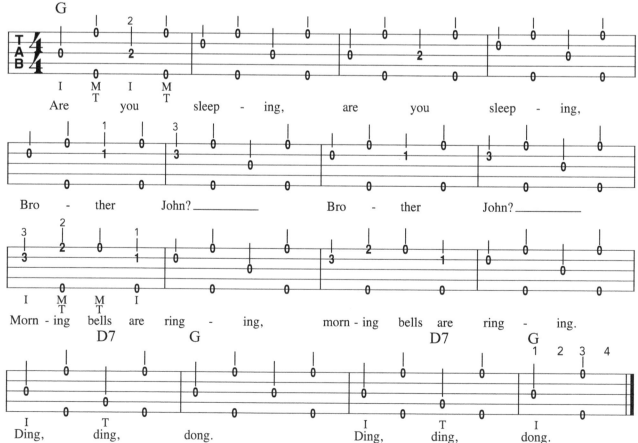

Rolls & Slides

Forward Roll

Bluegrass banjo playing is made up of *rolls*. Rolls are patterns for the picking hand. Your first roll is the *forward roll*. Below is one measure of the forward roll pattern. As you can see it's written using eighth notes, with eight notes fitting into a four-beat measure.

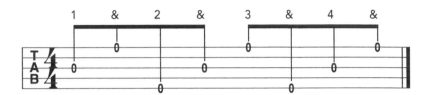

Here are four measures of the forward roll. Play them slowly and be extra careful to keep the rhythm smooth. Try to make it sound like a flowing river of notes. It will help to listen to the track on the audio and try to copy the sound.

Track 21

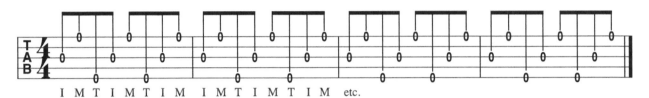

This time the index finger plays the B string instead of the G.

Track 22

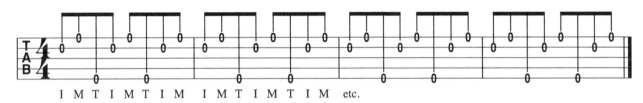

Now it's time for your first song using the forward roll! Again, when you see the C and D7 written above the staff, be sure to hold down the full chord with your fret hand, even if you're not playing all the notes in the chord.

Track 23

Rollin' Forward

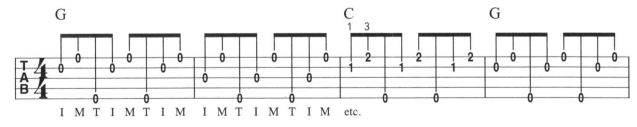

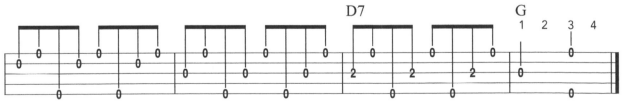

Our next song has been enjoyed by all kinds of people for well over 150 years! The tune combines the forward roll and pinches, eighth notes, and quarter notes. As usual, remember to hold down the entire C and D7 chords when they come up, even though not all their notes may be played. Be sure to see those quarter notes coming in measures 2, 4, 6, and 8, and let them ring for their full beat.

Track 24

Boil Those Cabbage Down

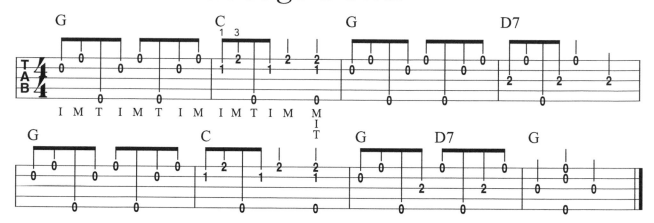

In "Red River Valley," the index finger plays the melody notes (the 1st, 4th, and 7th notes in most measures). To bring the melody out, be sure to let each of those notes ring as long as possible. If it's a fretted note, keep that fret-hand finger down until you play another note on that string. If it's a note on an open string then let it ring until you need to fret that string for another note.

Pickup Notes

A musical phrase may start on a beat other than the first one in a measure. When this happens at the beginning of a song like the one below, it is called a *pickup measure*. Count 1 and 2 silently, and play the first two notes on beats 3 and 4.

Track 25

Red River Valley

▶ Hold down the full shapes for the C and D7 chords when they come up.

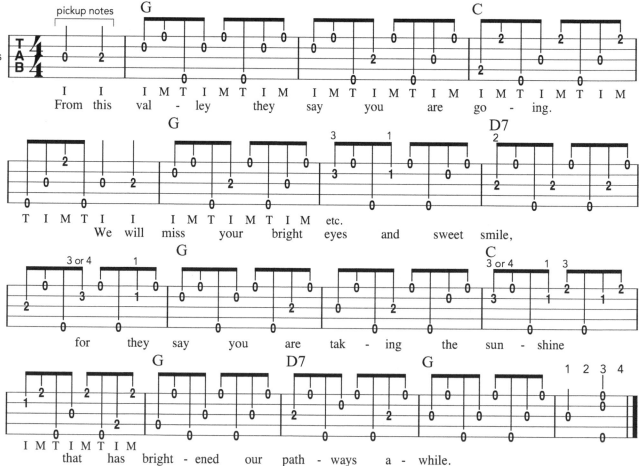

Music History

Also known as "Boil Them Cabbage Down," "Bile Dem Cabbage Down," or "Bake Them Hotcakes Down," this classic American folk song has unclear origins. Folklorist Alan Lomax asserts that the tune has roots reaching all the way to the African slaves brought to the southern United States.

The song "Red River Valley" is one of the most widespread of North American folk songs. Its melody has been traced back to a ditty from the state of New York, "The Bright Mohawk Valley," which was published in 1896. The Red River Valley in this tune is likely the northern one found in Manitoba, Canada.

Inside-Outside Roll

Now it's time to add a new pick-hand roll to the mix. The name *inside-outside* describes the picking pattern. Pick two of the inside strings, and then the two outside strings on your banjo. To get the pattern in your mind it may help to say "inside, outside" in rhythm as you play the measures below.

I Got the GBGD'S

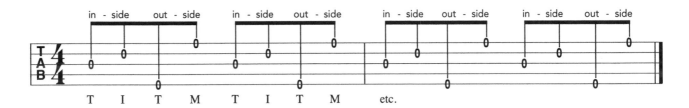

Here is the same pattern, with the thumb playing the low D string.

Now I Got the DBGD'S!

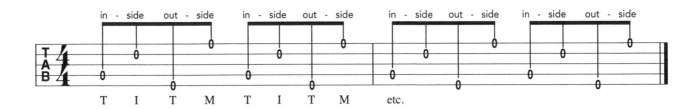

Now try a combination of the two inside-outside rolls.

Inside-Outside Combo

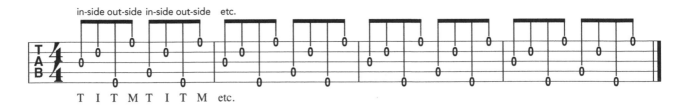

Let's put this new roll to work! We'll start with a tune we learned before, "Goodnight Ladies," which we played with pinches only. Adding the roll gives it more rhythmic interest.

Make sure you pay attention to the "2" above the staff in the first measure. Fret that note with the 2nd finger of the fret hand. When the finger lets go of the note, keep it close to the string, ready to play. Watch the right hand in measure 6; you're holding two strings down at the 5th fret.

Track 30

Goodnight Ladies
(with Inside-Outside Roll)

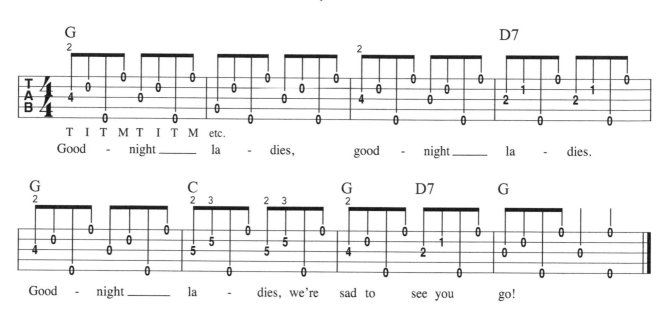

The different rolls work together to create a variety of sounds all in the same tune. Variation makes a tune more enjoyable to both play and hear. This tune combines the forward roll and the inside-outside roll.

Track 31

Go Tell Aunt Rhody

► Practice the 2nd measure as a round (over and over in rhythm) to get used to starting the forward roll with the thumb.

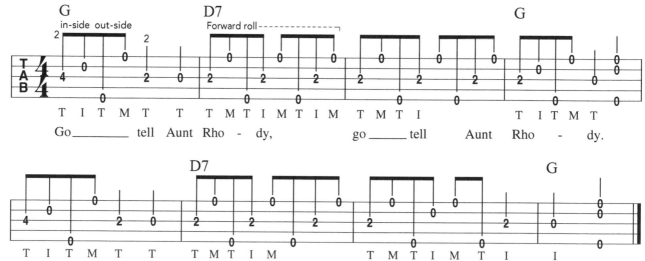

Sometimes a composer (or a teacher) will put *measure numbers* on the music to make it easy to point out which ones need practice. The pickup measure, if there is one, is usually not counted in the numbering scheme.

Practice measure 3 alone, and when it feels smooth, play measures 2 and 3 together as a "round"— over and over with no break in the rhythm.

Track 32

Will the Circle Be Unbroken

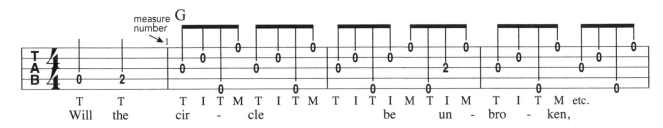

In measure 6, hold down the C chord and move the second finger only for the fifth note in that measure.

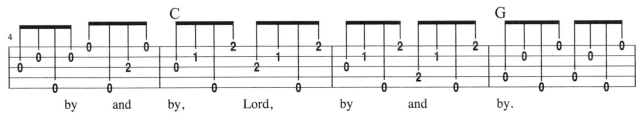

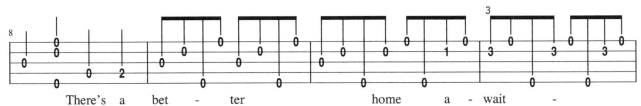

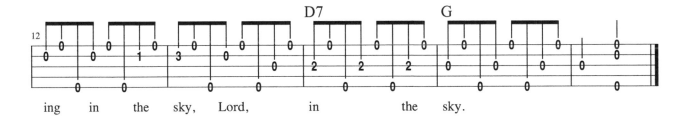

Track 33

The Slide

Of all banjo techniques, *slides* perhaps come closest to mimicking the human voice. They are a powerful tool for bringing variation to a tune. Slides are sounded by the fret hand without being picked, and are indicated in music by lines between the notes. Sometimes you'll also see an *sl* under the line.

When playing the following measures, only pick the string on beats 1, 2, 3, and 4. The notes on the "ands" are created by the fret-hand slide. All slides in the following examples are played with the 2nd finger of the fret hand. These need to sound as even eighth notes. As you count "1 and 2 and 3 and 4 and," slide when you say "and." Be sure to listen to the audio track.

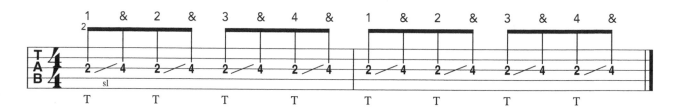

Now let's put slides into the inside-outside roll. The slide is the same as above, but now you also play the open B string at the end of your slide, on the "and." Play slowly and try to make the slide and the open note sound at the same time.

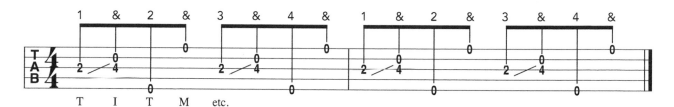

Goodnight Ladies
(Using Inside-Outside Roll, Pinches, and Slides)

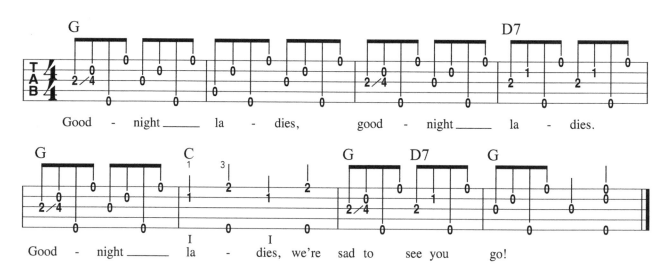

Here is a three-fret slide on the low D string, from the 2nd to the 5th fret. As in previous examples, make sure you're sliding in an even, steady rhythm. Be sure not to speed up. As you count "1 and 2 and 3 and 4 and," pick the string on beats 1, 2, 3, and 4. Slide (without picking) when you say "and."

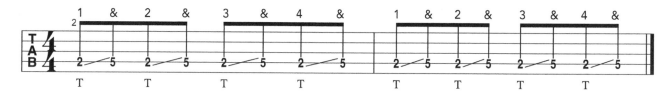

Now practice the sliding lick for the next tune by itself.

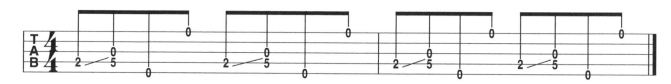

She'll Be Comin' 'Round the Mountain

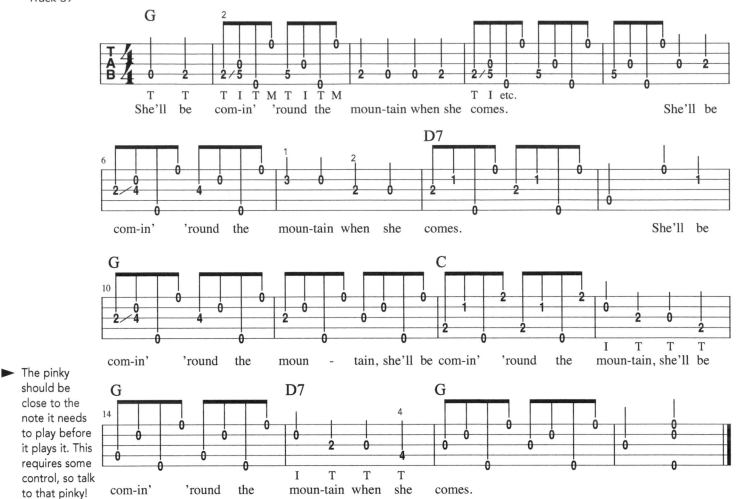

► The pinky should be close to the note it needs to play before it plays it. This requires some control, so talk to that pinky!

Repeat Signs and Numbered Endings

Repeat signs are double barlines with two dots, as shown in measures 1 and 4 of the next tune. Just as the name implies, repeat signs tell you to play certain passages twice. The brackets above the final two measures indicate *first* and *second endings* to the repeated section.

Here's what you do:

- Play the first line up to the repeat sign at the end of measure 4 (the first ending).
- Without missing a beat, go back to the first repeat sign at the beginning of measure 1.
- Play the first three measures, *skip measure 4*, and play measure 5 instead.
- Keep going, to the next line in this case.

"Old McDonald" combines the inside-outside roll, slides, pinches, and some single notes. Notice that some of the slides go from fret 2 to 4, while others go all the way from the 2nd to the 5th fret. The fourth measure has a little bass run on the D string. Note the fret-hand fingering. Listen closely to the audio track to get the timing of the slides right.

Old McDonald

Track 40

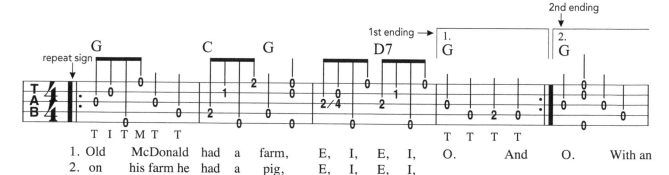

1. Old McDonald had a farm, E, I, E, I, O. And O. With an
2. on his farm he had a pig, E, I, E, I,

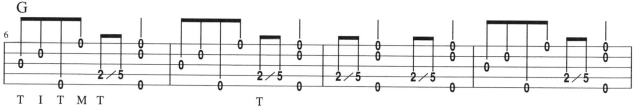

oink, oink here, and an oink, oink there, and here an oink, there an oink, ev-'ry-where an oink, oink.

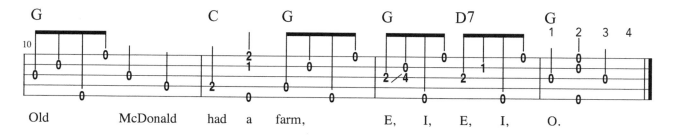

Old McDonald had a farm, E, I, E, I, O.

Music History

Like most folk songs, "Old McDonald" has parents. According to Mr. Doney Hammondtree, it likely came from an older song called "The Merry Green Fields of the Lowland" (Vince Randolph, Ozark Folksongs Vol. 3 No. 457) which he learned in 1900. The earliest official publication of "Old McDonald" is 1917, when it appeared in a book called *Tommy's Tunes*.

Our next picking pattern is the ***forward-reverse roll***.

Forward-Reverse Roll

Track 41

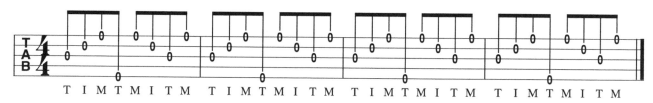

T I M T M I T M   T I M T M I T M   T I M T M I T M   T I M T M I T M

The following tune uses the forward-reverse roll all the way through to the last measure. Hold down the whole C and D7 chords. In measure 14, lift your index finger for the open B string.

Worried Man Blues

Track 42

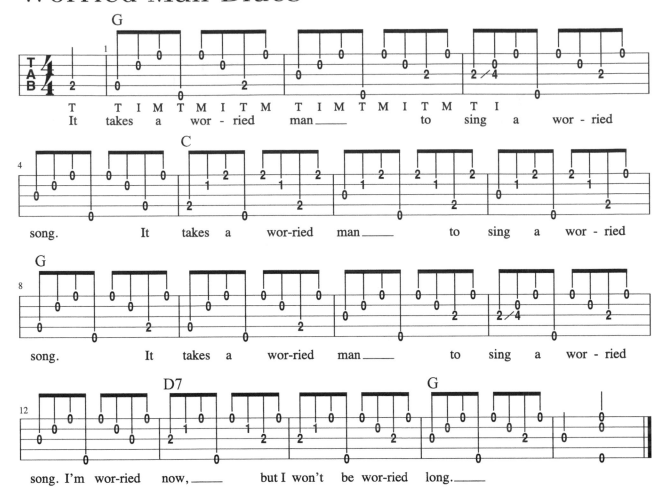

Music History

"Worried Man Blues" has become a standard in roots music repertoires, but its exact origins are lost in the mists of nineteenth-century folk music. Its famous opening line, "It takes a worried man to sing a wor-ried song," was popularized on records in 1930 when the Carter Family recorded it. Lester Flatt and Earl Scruggs recorded it in 1961.

This version of "Go Tell Aunt Rhody" combines the forward-reverse roll with slides and pinches.

Go Tell Aunt Rhody

Track 43

► In the 7th measure, keep the whole D7 chord pressed down, just lifting your index finger for the open B string note.

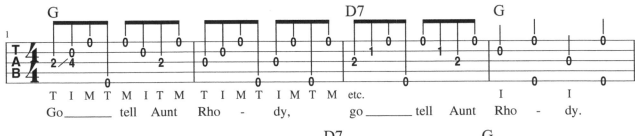

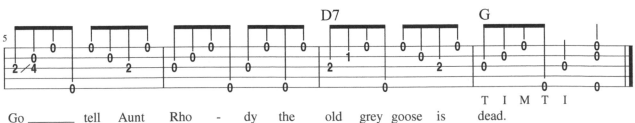

Lesson 4 | Pickin' a Classic

"Cripple Creek" starts with a pickup note on beat 4 that is slid into beat 1 of the first measure. Rehearse this slide as a repeating loop all by itself, counting aloud in even rhythm. Pick the note on beat 4 and slide it when you count beat 1: "1 2 3 pick, slide 2 3 pick, slide 2 3 pick, slide 2 3 pick, slide." Slide with your third finger on the D string. Notice the final slide goes over the repeat sign; it means that last note in measure 4 slides into the first measure. Match your sound to the audio. Once you play this, you're dipping a couple toes into Cripple Creek for sure!

Track 44

"Cripple Creek" Slide

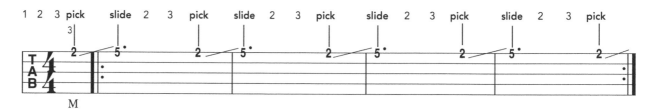

Measure 2 of "Cripple Creek" contains a forward-roll and pinch combination. Practice it until you can play it smoothly, and you're waist-deep in Cripple Creek at least!

Track 45

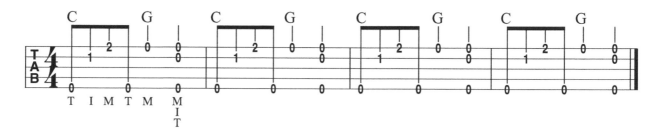

"Cripple Creek" originated as a fiddle tune. It has an "A" part (the first line) and a "B" part (the second line). Both parts are played twice. To end the tune, play the 1st ending of the "B" part. "Cripple Creek" is perhaps the single most popular tune to pick on the five-string banjo.

Track 46

Cripple Creek

► The 2nd ending of the "B" part is only played if you're continuing back to the "A" part. Play the 1st ending of the "B" part on the second time through the "B" part to end the tune.

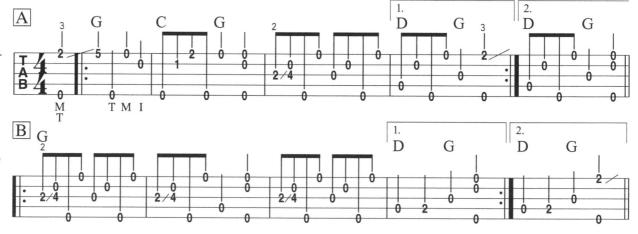

In the fourth and fifth measures of each section, there is a D chord indicated in the music, but you do not make a D chord here. All the strings are open. If someone were playing rhythm for you, that's where they would play a D.

Track 47

Hammer-Ons

In playing the banjo, some notes can be sounded by the fret hand without being picked, such as the slides you learned earlier. The second technique to work on for this is called the *hammer-on*.

Start with proper fret-hand position, keeping your thumb behind the neck. Pluck the open G string.

Hammer with the middle finger, *just behind* the fret. Hammer so that if the banjo neck weren't there, you'd hammer your finger straight into your thumb.

When you release the finger, keep it close to the strings (within 3/4 of an inch), as it needs to be ready to play again.

The key to clear hammer-ons is not strength. If you hammer straight into the fretboard and accurately (just behind the fret), you'll have strength to spare and get a nice-sounding hammered note.

A hammer-on is written with a curved *slur* mark. The thumb picks just the first note. The second is sounded by the fret-hand hammer-on.

It's Hammer Time!

Track 48

On the G string:

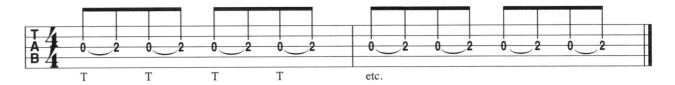

Try them on the D string:

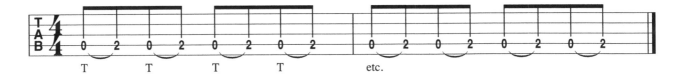

Now play the same hammer-ons, but add a picked note with the index finger. This note is played at the same time as you hammer. Picking one note while hammering another may feel strange at first, but go slowly and you'll get it!

Track 49

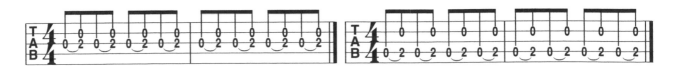

Practice hammer-ons with the inside-outside roll. Keep a steady rhythm.

Track 50

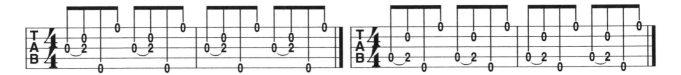

Now let's try "Cripple Creek" with some hammer-ons. To end the tune, play the 1st ending of the "B" part like on page 23.

Track 51

Cripple Creek

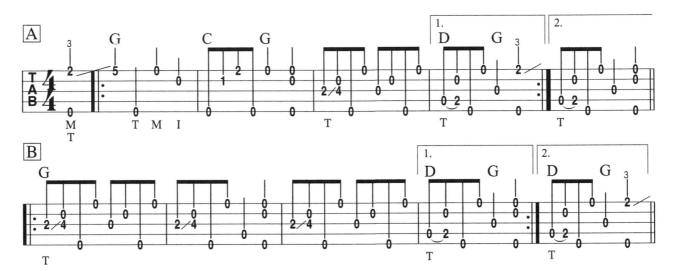

Pull-Offs

Track 52

A *pull-off* is another way for the fret hand to sound notes. Starting from a fretted note, the fret-hand finger flicks the string as it comes off, either pulling slightly toward the floor or pushing toward the ceiling. Practice it both ways. Either way, the sound of the lower note comes when the finger releases the string.

Play each of the following measures several times in a row in a nice steady rhythm.

Pull (down) and push (up) the G string.

Now pull and push that big D string.

Pull-offs and hammer-ons are both marked with curved slurs in the music.

Track 53

Pull-off in a Roll
(with a Pinch and a Slide)

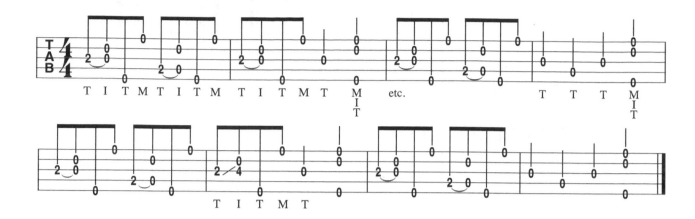

Here's a familiar song worked up with slides, hammer-ons, and pull-offs. As you can see, each hammered note is the second eighth note in a group of four. Hold down the hammered note while the rest of the notes in the group are played. For example, the hammer-on in the first measure is held down until you get to the first note of the second measure. In measure 14, after the slide, be sure to hold down the 2nd finger (on the 2nd fret) while the pinky plays its note on the 4th fret of the low D string.

Track 54

She'll Be Comin' 'Round the Mountain

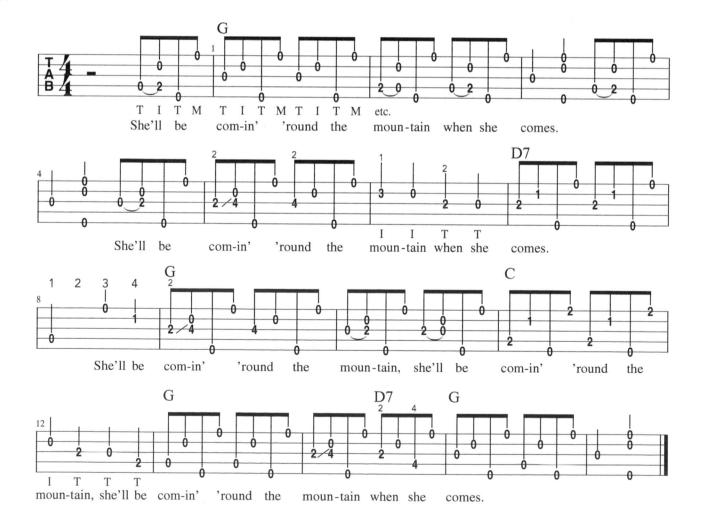

Lesson 5 | A Big Lick

Track 55

This quintessential Earl Scruggs bluegrass banjo lick, once learned, can be used again and again in countless tunes! It's one of the ABCs of bluegrass banjo. Before trying the lick, first play this exercise, picking the high D string as you slide. Remember to count "1 and 2 and 3 and 4 and" and slide when you say "and."

▶ Take your time, and make sure you use the correct picking-hand fingers!

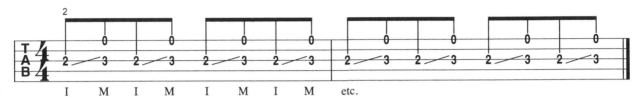

This version of "She'll Be Comin' Round the Mountain" uses our new lick in measure 3, and also mixes in some different rolls. The Scruggs lick also appears as a nice ending in measure 15. In measure 7, we insert a forward-reverse roll for the D7. In measure 14, the two notes after the slide are both held down until the first note of the next measure.

Track 56

She'll Be Comin' 'Round the Mountain

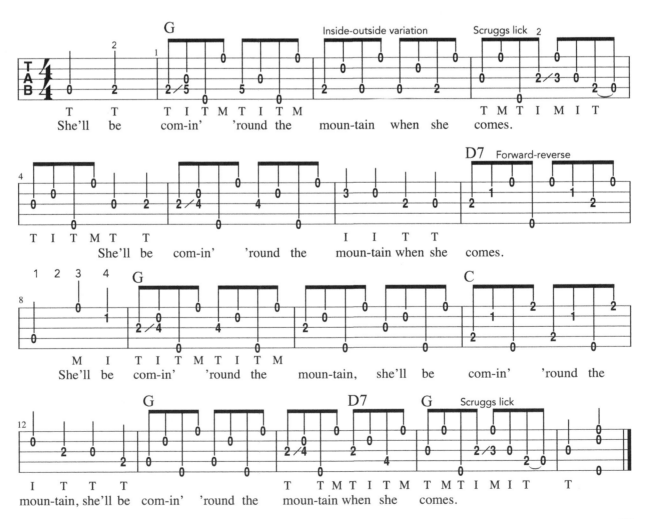

27

To get the feel for the picking in measure 12 of "Walkin' Cane," play these pretty notes several times.

Track 57

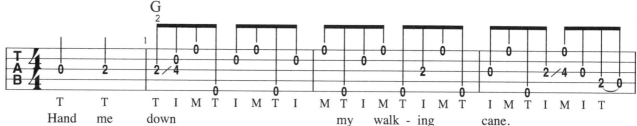

Watch the picking for the Scruggs lick; it starts with the index finger. In measure 6, there's a variation on the forward roll. It's similar to measure 2 in "Will the Circle Be Unbroken." In that same measure, notice the first note is picked with the thumb.

Track 58

Walkin' Cane

► The slide in the Scruggs licks in this arrangement slides all the way to the 4th fret instead of the 3rd. Compare the different sounds between the two!

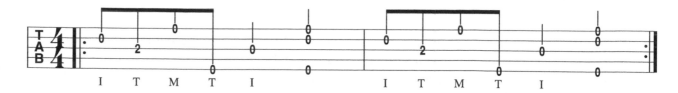
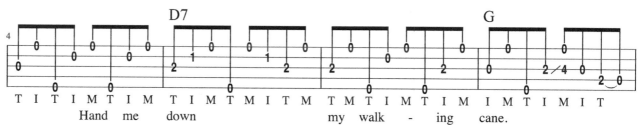
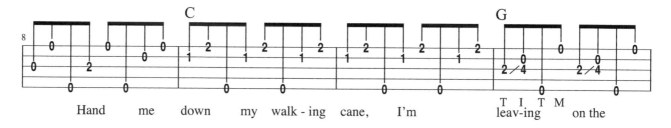
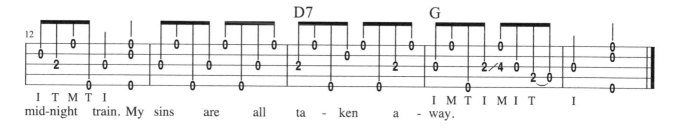

Music History

Gid Tanner and His Skillet Lickers first recorded "Hand Me Down My Walking Cane" in 1926. Gid Tanner was one of the most widely-recognized names among country music enthusiasts of the 1920s and 1930s, and the Skillet Lickers were one of the most influential string bands during the formative years of the country music industry.

Note Names

The musical alphabet uses seven letters, from A–G, to name notes and chords. The lowest note on the banjo is the 4th-string D, with the other letters following in alphabetical order up the neck, until you reach another D note at the 12th fret. At that fret, the series starts over.

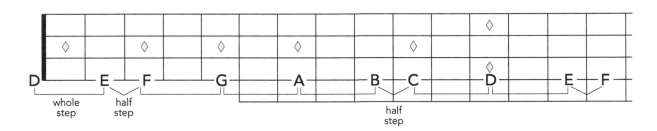

Most of the letters are two frets apart. This distance is called a **whole step**. From E to F, and from B to C, we have **half steps**, notes that are only one fret apart. This fact means that it's not necessary to memorize the name of the every note on the neck right away. Just start by remembering the names of the open strings, and that B–C and E–F are half steps, one fret apart.

The unlabeled notes are named by using the words **sharp** (♯) or **flat** (♭) in relation to the note immediately below or above. For example, the first fret on the string may either be called D♯, because it is a half step above D, or **E♭**, because it is a half step below E. Which name is correct depends on the scale or key the note is used in at the time. For now, we can name these notes either way.

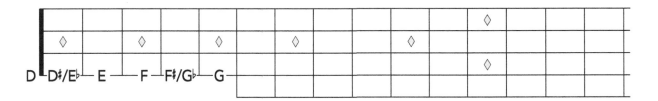

The alphabet starts from G on the 3rd string, again with half steps from B–C and E–F, reaching another G at the 12th fret.

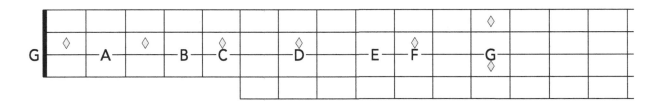

The B string goes up to another B at the 12th fret, with a C right on fret 1. That's the **root** of our C chord.

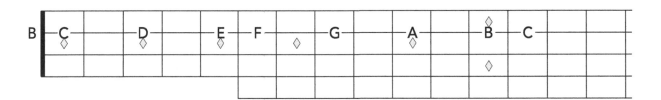

The 1st string is an open D note, the same pitch as found on the 12th fret of string 4. Its notes are the same as on the 4th string, but an *octave* (eight letters) higher.

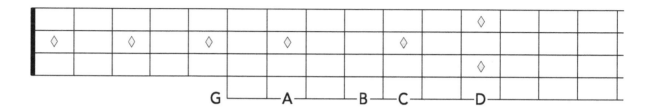

The short G string is the same as the 1st string from fret 5 up. Advanced banjoists make use of this knowledge as they play high up on the neck. As beginners, we're only using this string as an open *drone* note, the characteristic banjo sound.

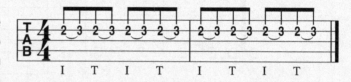

It will help to be familiar with note names for the next lesson on chords, so review this section a few times before then.

Track 59

A New Hammer-On

Thus far, all of the hammer-ons you've played have been from an open string to a fretted note. Now we will hammer from one fretted note to another. Start with your index finger on the second fret.

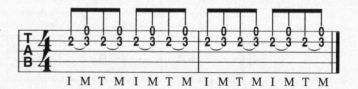

Keep it down throughout. Pick this note, then hammer on with the second finger. Hammer just behind the fret as always. Alternate between picking the starting note with your index finger and thumb as indicated.

Now we'll add the open D string. Hammer the B string just as you pick the D string; not before.

Now play this complete phrase several times with even rhythm. We owe Earl Scruggs a big thanks for this popular hammer-on lick.

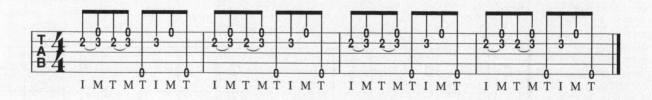

In the next tune, watch for the quarter notes in measures 4 and 5—no running stop signs! In measure 6, from the D7 chord move the 2nd finger only for the note on the low D string.

Train 45

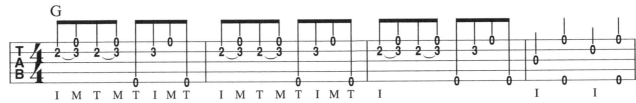

► All the notes in the last line are fretted with the 2nd finger.

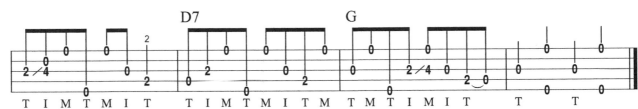

In "Goin' Down That Road Feelin' Bad," the pickup measure is a classic *lead-in* starting on beat 2. Besides starting tunes, it can start solos or *breaks* within tunes. This tune also includes your first *double tag* ending. This ending can be used to end other tunes as well.

Goin' Down That Road Feelin' Bad

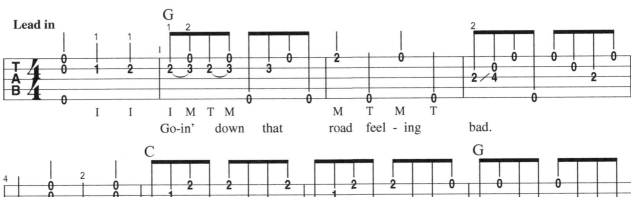

► In measures 5–6 and 9–10, move only your second finger for the note change during the C chord. Leave all other fingers down.

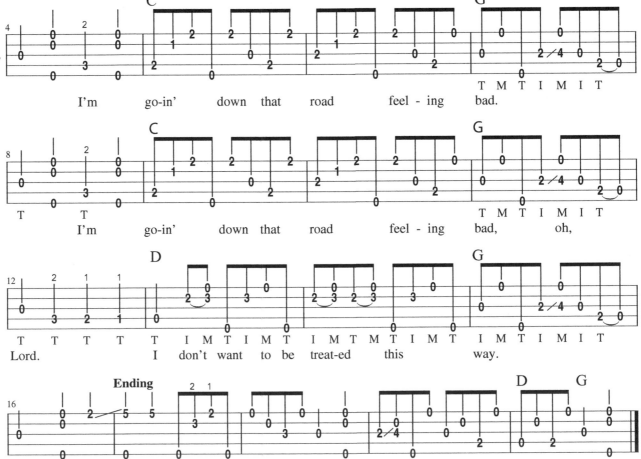

Major Chords

If you look at individual musicians in any ensemble, be it a bluegrass, rock, or jazz band, you'll find that each player spends the majority of time playing a supporting, or **backup** part. In rock music it may be called playing rhythm, which backs up the lead. When someone is singing or when someone else is playing a solo, the banjoist often backs them up with the chords for the song.

We've learned three chords thus far: G, C, and D7. We've learned them in open position, where each chord uses some open (unfretted) strings. (The G chord actually uses all open strings!) Now it's time to learn to play **major chords** (those represented by a letter name only) in closed position. As the name implies, there are no open strings when playing closed-position chords. These are essential to playing basic backup rhythm.

Learn Your FDAs (Banjo Vitamins)

There are only three closed major chord shapes on the banjo. Each of these three shapes is moveable to anyplace on the neck. Where a shape is played determines the name of the chord. In the diagrams below, the root note of each chord shape is circled. As you learn each shape, focus on the root so that you'll know which chord (A, B, C, etc.) the shape is producing when played at a particular fret.

First, we have the **F shape**, named after the chord this shape produces when played at the third fret, with the root under the ring finger. This is a new shape for us, using all four fret-hand fingers. A closed-position G major chord using the F shape is shown here. The root is played by your ring finger on fret 5. Play the chord, then lift all your fingers to check that it sounds similar to the open-position G chord that you already know (the one with the open strings). Move this same shape up towards the banjo head by two frets, and you're now playing an A chord.

Thumb Test

As you practice, give each chord the **thumb test**. Hold down the chord shape and pick each string with the thumb, one at a time. If a note sounds muted or if it buzzes, look at the fretting hand and find the finger responsible for that note. Is it correctly placed on the right string and pressing down sufficiently? If the answer is "yes," and there's still a problem, then perhaps another finger is leaning into (and muting) the problem string. Keep the fingers arched!

▶ Move it down to the third fret, and it's an F major chord.

G
(F Shape)

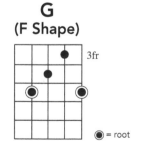

3fr

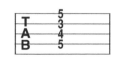

◉ = root

Next is the **D shape**. It's named after the chord the shape produces when played at the fourth fret, with the root on the 2nd string, fret 3. Here is a closed-position D chord using the D shape.

► This D chord becomes an E chord if you move it up two frets.

D
(D Shape)

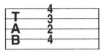

Finally, there's the **A shape**, named after the closed-position, second-fret A chord (also called the *barre* shape). Here is a closed-position C chord using the A shape. The root is on the 3rd string. Keep the finger straight and check that all the tones ring. No bent bar here!

► This shape becomes a D chord if you move it up to the 7th fret.

C
(A Shape)

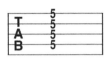

Play each of these chord shapes in various places on the neck and hear the huge variety of sounds just three shapes can make! To name the various chords, remember (and listen for) which note in the shape is the chord root, and if necessary, review **Lesson 6—Note Names**.

Once you get the hang of each chord shape it's time get that pick hand involved. The measures below show one of the most common pick-hand patterns for backup (also called **accompaniment**), using the open G chord.

Track 63

Backup Pattern

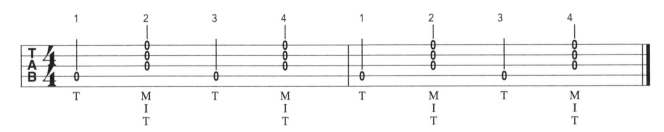

The next step is to hold each closed-position chord shape down while picking this pattern. Play each measure several times.

Track 64

G (F shape)   D (D shape)   C (A shape)

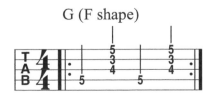
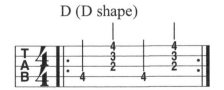
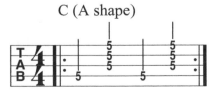

Changing Chords

When changing from G to D, the index and middle fingers exchange strings: the index goes to the middle finger's string and the middle finger goes to the index finger's string. Focus your attention on either finger and visualize where it needs to go, and the other finger will move to its new home naturally.

Let's practice this part of the chord move alone. We'll call this part the *flip*. Play this *very slowly*. The pinky and ring fingers stay on their same strings. Don't lift them at all.

For the complete chord change, just relax the grip and slide the hand down one fret. You're not going for the sound of a slide here, just economy of motion. The movement of fingers as you change from chord to chord should be as efficient as possible. Don't lift a finger more than is necessary.

Now add this slide before the flip. Play slowly. Repeat.

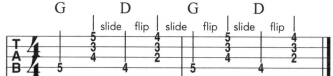

Here's another tip to smooth out the chord change: you needn't plant all the fingers at once. The first note for each chord is played by itself, so you can flip the fingers during the time that note is being played. Pluck the chord, then loosen the grip as you slide to the next low note and press it down. Then flip the others into place.

Now let's practice the change from G to C. While holding your hand on the G chord, focus on your index finger only. Visualize its move up to the 5th fret for the A-shape C. Conversely, when you're playing the C chord, have the ring finger in your mind, as it's the first finger you'll need to put down when returning to G.

You can plant the other fingers to complete the G chord while the ring-finger note is being played. You don't need to lay the whole G chord down at once.

Backup Accents

There are four beats to each measure for everything in this book. This is called a **4/4 time signature**. Beats 1 and 3 are downbeats, and beats 2 and 4 are called **upbeats**. When playing backup it's usually a good idea to play louder on (or **accent**) the upbeats. In the following example, the pinches in the backup pattern are on the upbeats, so you play those a bit louder. However, you can't play louder than the singer or soloist, as your job is to support them.

Muting

A good way to create accents and have your playing heard in the proper way is to *mute* the strings. This gives the sound a nice punch, or pop, and prevents the strings from ringing too loudly. After you play the pinch part of your backup picking pattern, relax the fretting-hand fingers so they're barely touching the strings. This stops the strings from ringing. Pick the strings, then let up the pressure to mute. Listen to the audio track and try to imitate its sound.

Track 67

Goodnight Ladies Backup

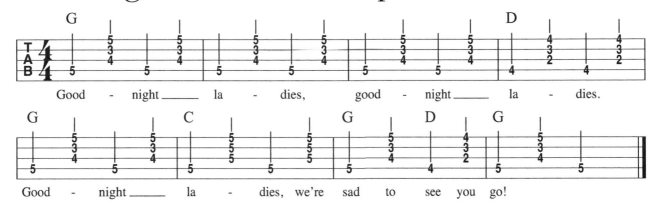

Reading Chord Charts

Throughout this book there are chord names (G, C, D7) written in the music. These have two functions:

1. They tell you which open-position chord to hold down with the fret hand when playing the arrangements of the songs.

2. They also tell you which closed-position shapes to use for playing a backup part to the songs. Instead of reading the notes given on the staff, count your way through the measures and play the given chord using the backup picking pattern. This is using the music as a *chord chart*.

Here's a chord chart for "Cripple Creek." Only the chord names are written. You have to count! There are four beats per measure, which in your pattern equals thumb, pinch, thumb, pinch.

Notice the 2nd and 4th measures have a chord change in the middle. Change chords on beat 3. Use the slide-and-flip technique for the change in measure 4. All other chords change on the first beat.

Track 68

Cripple Creek Chord Chart

► When reading a chart, look ahead to see what chord is coming so you'll be ready for it.

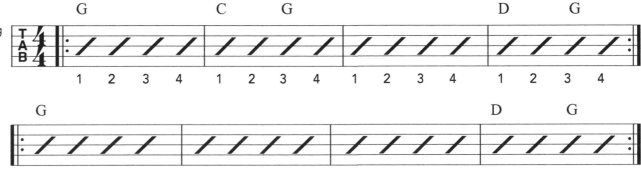

Now that you know the basic backup pattern, you can practice backing up all the tunes on the audio! When you read the tunes as chord charts, you'll notice a D7 chord is often used, as that's the position your fret hand needs to be in when playing the written lead part. When playing backup, however, use the closed-position D chord we learned when you see a D7 in the music.

Sixteenth-Note Licks

The new aspect to this slide lick is that the slide itself is faster. It's written in *sixteenth notes*. Two sixteenth notes equal the duration of an eighth note. Listen to the example on the audio, and keep your foot tapping the same steady quarter-note beat as always when imitating it.

In tablature we have fret numbers instead of the noteheads used in standard notation.

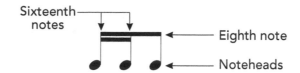

Be sure to start your slide just behind the 2nd fret. Dig in a little bit and be sure you can hear the sound of the finger sliding over the 2nd fret.

Track 69

Sixteenth-Note Slides

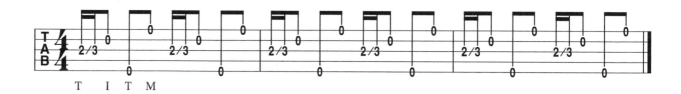

Track 70

A New Pull-Off

Here's a new pull-off lick using sixteenth notes. As with previous pull-offs, practice the licks below two ways: one, pulling off toward the floor, and two, pushing off toward the ceiling.

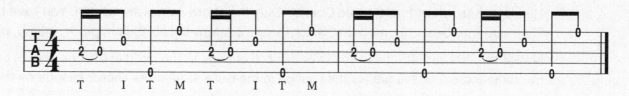

Now combine the sixteenth-note slides and pull-offs.

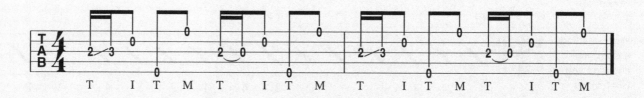

Make sure all the notes (especially the sixteenths) are clearly audible. How should they sound? Listen to the audio track!

Once you get the hang of these licks, you're ready for a full-blown Earl Scruggs version of "Cripple Creek." This is full-steam-ahead bluegrass!

End the tune by playing the 1st ending of the "B" part, like in the other versions of "Cripple Creek" in this book.

Track 71

Cripple Creek

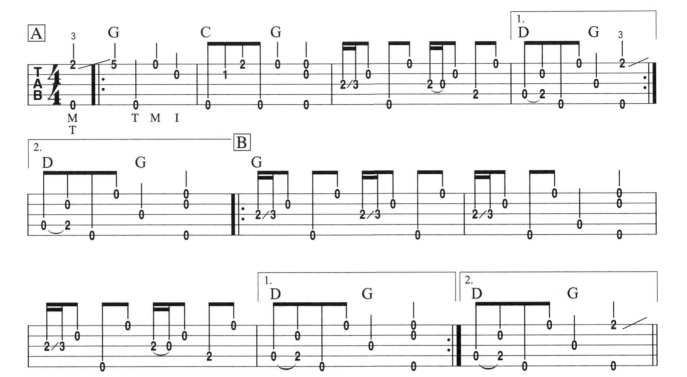

Pullin' Off a New Pull-Off

Track 72

Let's get ready for the next lick by practicing pull-offs to a fretted note instead of an open string. Keep the index finger down, and make sure you play a smooth rhythm of even eighth notes.

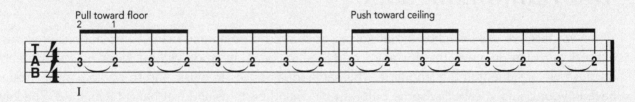

Now we'll play the fretted pull-offs as sixteenth notes, as part of a roll. Be sure the index finger is down by the time you pull off.

Nine-Pound Hammer
(Puttin' in the Pull-Off)

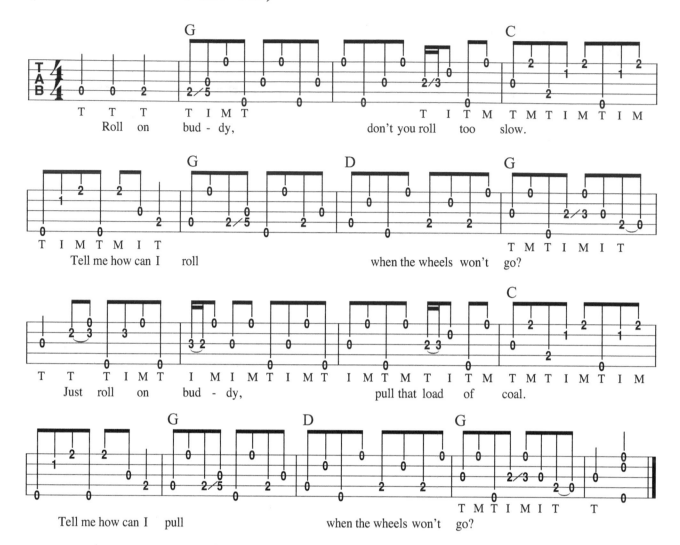

The Banjo Language

When we talk, we use inflection in our voices, and can choose among many combinations of words that express our ideas in a way that fits any mood or situation. This we do without needing to think about it, because we are fluent in the language. This same idea applies to music and to banjo playing. You now have in your banjo vocabulary some different pick-hand patterns and fret-hand techniques. The key to becoming fluent with them is to use them!

The Capo

A *capo* is a good friend to the banjo player, especially those who play in the bluegrass style. It raises the pitch of the open strings. Most guitar capos will work on a banjo, but it's best to get a banjo capo. They're available at most music stores.

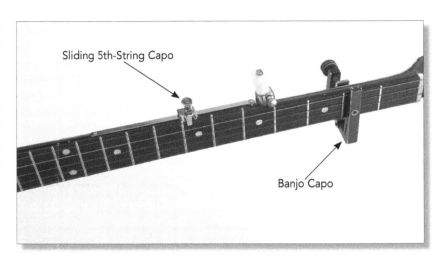

Sliding 5th-String Capo

Banjo Capo

Why Use One?

Capos enable the banjoist to play in different keys without changing their fingering. To be able to play in different keys is essential. For instance, a vocalist may want to sing in the key of C, or a fiddler may want to play a tune in D or A. While the banjo as an instument can accommodate any key, the bluegrass style relies on the effect of open strings. To preserve those open strings in different keys, a capo is at times a necessity.

Track 74

Putting It On

The capo should be put on just behind the fret (the same place you'd put your fingers), and should be snug enough so all the strings sound clear when strummed open. If it's too tight, it will pull the strings out of tune. If it's too loose, the strings will buzz.

Most banjoists have "railroad spikes" installed on the necks of their banjos. These are very small L-shaped hooks behind the 7th, 9th, and sometimes the 10th fret, under the short G string. Hooking the string under one raises its pitch. A qualified individual only should install these! Another solution for the 5th string is a sliding 5th-string capo (as shown in the photo).

If you have a capo, place it at the 2nd fret to play the following tune in A, and hook or capo the short G string at the 7th fret. You can also tune the short string up to A. Though usually played in A, "Old Joe Clark" can also be played in G without a capo.

When reading the tablature, all fretted notes are read in relation to the capo. For example, a "2" means two frets higher than the capo fret, which is now "0." The written G chord will sound as an A.

If you are playing with another instrumentalist, he or she must transpose the chords. A guitarist may use a capo or transpose the music.

"Old Joe Clark" also uses the F chord that the F shape is named after. Slide your familiar closed-position G chord down so that your index finger is at the first fret (relative to the capo) and you have the F chord.

Old Joe Clark

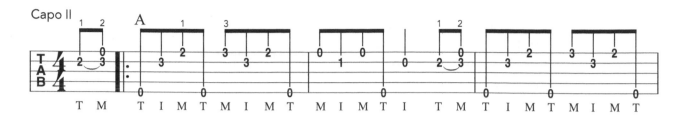

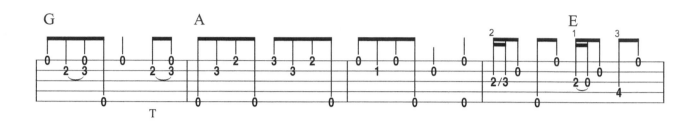

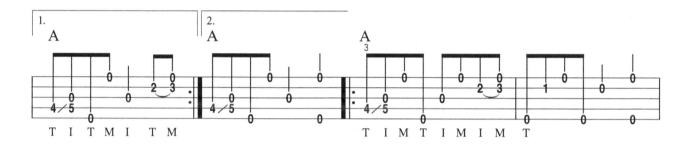

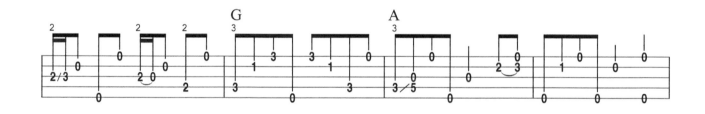

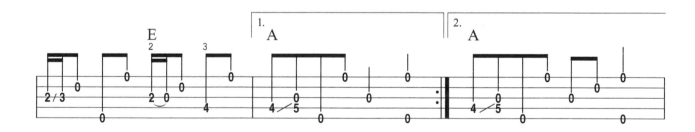

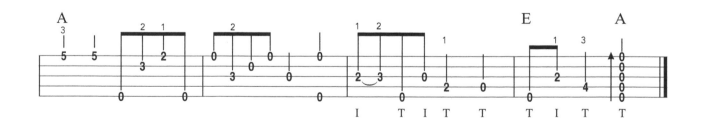

Backward Roll

Track 76

The *backward roll* is the exact reverse of the forward roll.

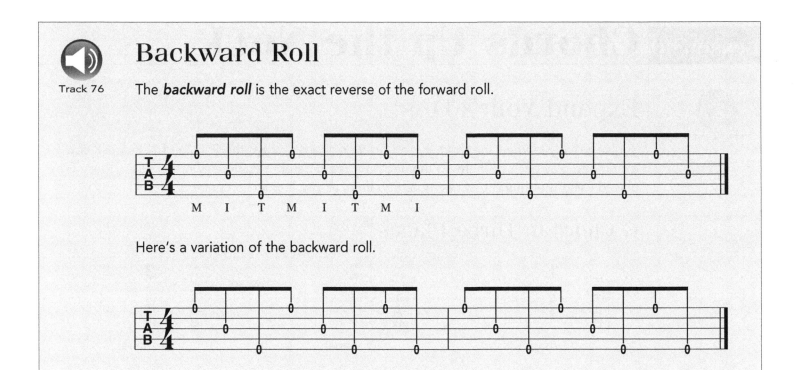

Here's a variation of the backward roll.

Playing Up the Neck

So far, all of your playing has taken place up to the 5th fret, unless you used a capo. As you can well see, there's a whole neck to use. Let's crack it open a bit! The following high break uses the variation of the backward roll and 2nd zone partial chord shapes. We'll talk more about these after you enjoy the following melodious sounds.

Boil Those Cabbage Down

Track 77

► Pay close attention to the fret-hand fingering (1, 2, 3, or 4 above the music)!

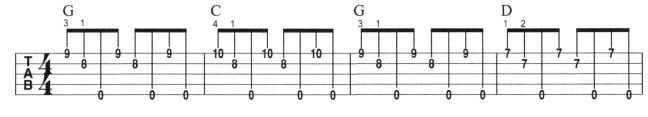

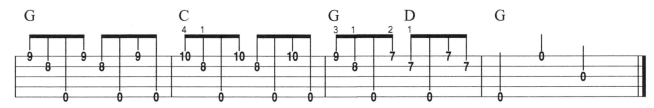

"Boil Those Cabbage Down" sounds pretty as a duet if you have someone else play the low version.

41

Chords Up the Neck

Track 78

Expand Your FDAs!

You've already learned the three closed-position chord shapes, the F, D, and A shapes. Now it's time to play each of them up the neck in three different locations. On the audio, these are played using the thumb test one note at a time, as you learned on page 32.

G Chord in Three Places

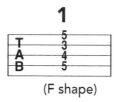

(F shape)

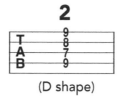

(D shape)

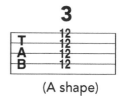

(A shape)

C Chord in Three Places

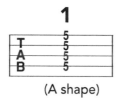

(A shape)

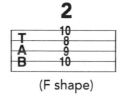

(F shape)

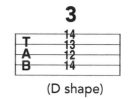

(D shape)

D Chord in Three Places

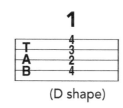

(D shape)

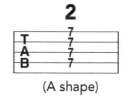

(A shape)

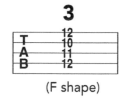

(F shape)

Track 79

Now it's time to play each chord in three places using the backup picking pattern. Take it very slow and try to envision the first note of the next chord before going to it! (They're circled.)

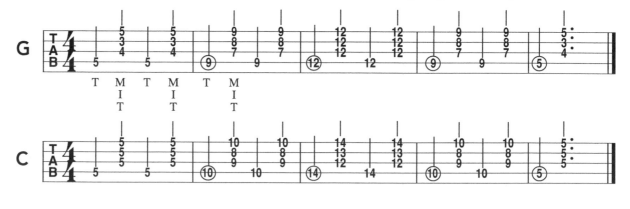

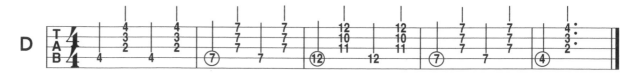

Three Chord Zones

Here's how you can play G–C–D–G in three "zones" on the neck. Notice you use the same three chord shapes in each zone, in a different order, and for a different chord.

Track 80

Zone One

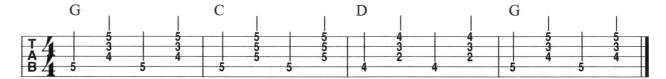

Track 81

Zone Two

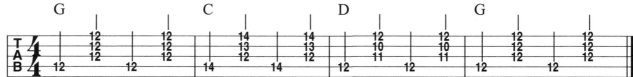

Track 82

Zone Three

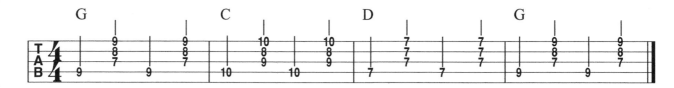

Backup Tips

1. When playing backup say the name of the chord to yourself (or aloud).
2. Play each chord (G, C, and D) in each of its three places on the neck.
3. Play backup using each position. When each position feels somewhat familiar, experiment with combining them. For example, play the progression G–C–D–G like this:

Track 83

Zone-to-Zone Backup

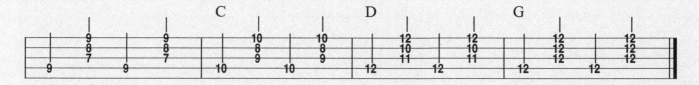

What have you done? You have now played the G, C, and D chords using each closed chord shape!

This tune is commonly played in the key of A, with a capo on the 2nd fret. The only full chord you hold down is the F in measure 3 and first half of measure 4. The 2nd finger plays the pull-offs. The other fret-hand fingers (holding down the F chord) don't move. In measure 11, hold down the top two strings of the F chord.

Salt River (Salt Creek)

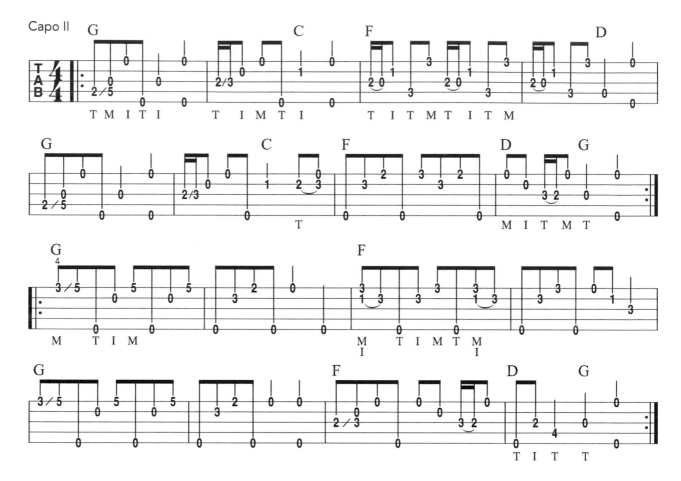

Music History

"Salt River" is an example of how a traditional tune gets a new name, which then gains acceptance through popular use. Old-time players call this fiddle tune by its original name, "Salt River." "Salt River" probably refers to the river by that name in Kentucky. Bill Monroe and His Bluegrass Boys recorded this fiddle tune in 1964 under the title "Salt Creek," in honor of the creek in Indiana near where Monroe held his annual Bean Blossom Festival. Bluegrass pickers have since come to know it as "Salt Creek." Bill Keith, Monroe's banjoist at the time, apparently got the tune originally from West Virginia banjoist Don Stover. The Monroe recording gave this tune a new lease on life in the bluegrass circuit.

Single Eighth Notes

A single eighth note carries a **flag**, compared to the multiple eighth notes we've seen with *beams* joining their stems. Just like each beamed eighth note, a single flagged eighth note lasts for half a beat.

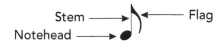

Stem ⟶ ◀ Flag
Notehead ⟶

In tablature, we have fret numbers instead of the noteheads used in standard notation.

Track 85

Dotted Notes

When you see a **dot** after a note, the duration of that note is increased by one half of its value. A quarter note gets one beat; a dotted quarter gets one and a half beats. When a dotted quarter note starts a measure, the note after it must fall on the *upbeat* (or "and") of 2.

You will rarely see dotted notes in banjo music; however, they'll make an appearance in "Hava Nagila!"

Track 86

C Minor Chord

"Hava Nagila" on the next page uses the C minor chord. It's a close relative of the open-position C major chord you already know. Lower both E notes (on strings 1 and 4) to E-flat at the 1st fret to change C major to C minor. You'll have to flip the 1st and 2nd fingers to switch to this chord from C major. More on minor chords in Lesson 12.

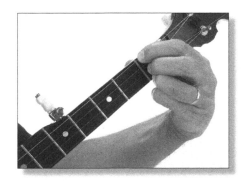

Cm

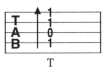

Single-String Picking

This is when you play the same string two or more times in a row. All notes are played with the thumb and index finger. When single-string picking, do not deviate from the T I picking pattern! It will feel strange for a while but you'll get used to it.

So Far Away

Track 87

▶ In measures 5 and 6, use the two fret-hand fingers indicated. Don't jump with one finger between strings.

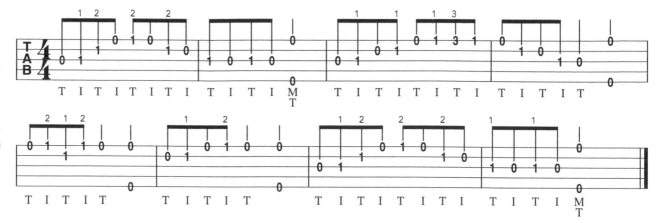

Hava Nagila

Track 88

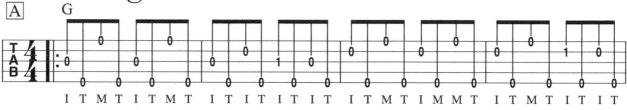

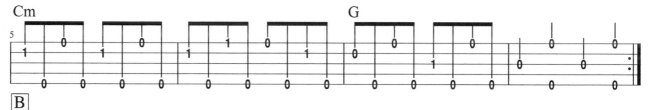

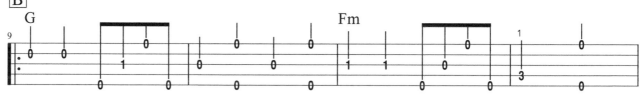

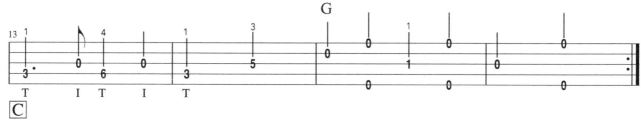

▶ In measures 22 and 24, from beat 3 to beat 4 is called "crossing under"; be sure to follow the right-hand fingerings indicated.

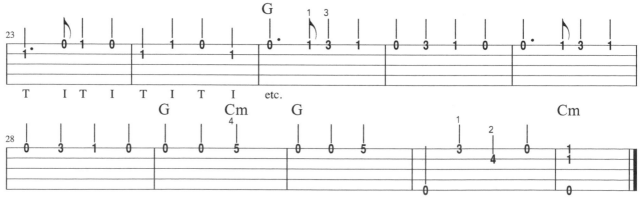

Minor Chords & Major Scales

Minor Chords

The three closed-position chord shapes you've learned are major chords. Major chords become *minor chords* by lowering one note. To change from C major to C minor, we lowered the E's to E-flats. In music theory, the 3rd of the chord is the note that's lowered to change from major to minor. As a beginner, you just need to learn the minor shapes and relate them to the major ones.

The change to minor requires rearranging the fingering of the chords, so be sure to read the fingering given below the diagrams. When you have them fingered correctly, play each one with the muted backup pattern, and try some rolls as well. Although only one note is changed, the minor chord is immediately recognizable and very different-sounding from its major counterpart.

Track 89

Major Chord Shape

Minor Chord Shape

 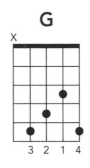
G
3 2 1 4

Gm
3 1 1 4

 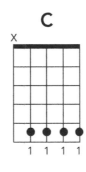
C
1 1 1 1

 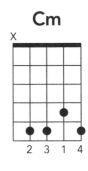
Cm
2 3 1 4

D
3 1 2 4

 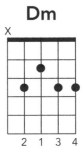
Dm
2 1 3 4

Although only one song in this book ("Hava Nagila") uses a minor chord, you'll come across more songs that use them. Some popular tunes that use minor chords are "Shady Grove," "Foggy Mountain Breakdown," "Jerusalem Ridge," and "Devil's Dream."

Major Scales

Scales are the palette from which come melodies. It's a great idea to become acquainted with scales, as they will enhance your overall musicianship. By playing these consistently over time, you'll develop your ear and be able to play a melody by hearing it. You'll also develop dexterity and technique.

G Major Open Position

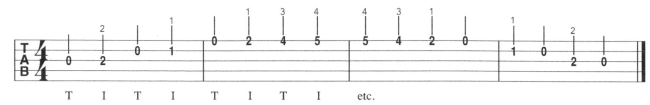

G Major Closed Position 1

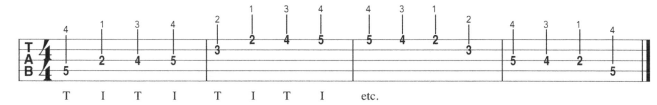

Scale shapes that do not include open strings can be moved to any key. For example, to play an A major scale, start this shape from fret 7.

G Major Closed Position 2

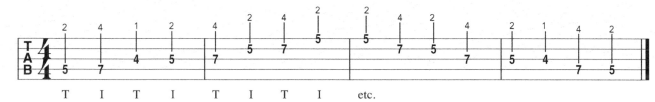

Melodic Style

The bluegrass "filler-note" approach is not used in the melodic (also called "Keith," or *arpa*) style. Rather, each note is more likely to be a melody note. One distinct feature of this style is that the notes are played *across* the strings. No string is played twice in a row, and this is what gives the melodic style a flowing and sometimes harp-like sound. This approach was devised by Bill Keith, whose efforts allowed fingerpicking banjo players to tackle fiddle tunes.

G Major Scale, Melodic Style 1

G Major Scale, Melodic Style 2

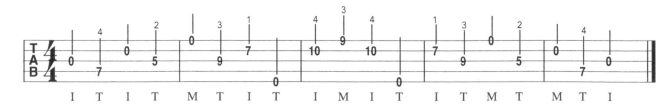